Knowing the Zairians (Congolese's)

2018

Edition: Baba Matandu ne Ngalula

BABABA

BENDE (ADAM)

MBUYI TSHIAME (EVE)

KOLE –A-BAYEMBI

KOLE-A-TSHILONDA

KOLE MUANA

KOLE TSHIFUKILE .... **KOLE W0T0**

SHABA	EQUATEUR
KASAI	BANDUNDU
BANDUNDU	KASAI
	HAUTKONGO
BANZAKONGO	BANZAKONGO
BATEKE	BOLOBO
KIVU	
HAUTKONGO	

BENA KOLE

CAPTER ONE: DO YOU KNOW ZAIRIAN MEN?

In this study we are on foot, according to the traits that are distributed more easily in a group or another, a ranking of Zairian in certain modes.

We found after following types: The Mungala the Muluba the Mukongo the Muyaka, the Shwahili, and Shabien. The men traits or types are no mre than women traits. The women accuse more type traits than men. This comes from the men characters to import the foreign women as wives in the Country; many students, soldiers, diplomats, and others bring their foreign wives in Kongo, these wives keep their original traits that accuse the difference and aspect in the Kongo. Even thouh, we give these foreign traits, the name of Kongolese local where they are living. This is the type of some traits in Shaba, Kasai, Bakongo, Kisangani.

It should be noted according to some aspects, others confuse, and form the same type than others.

A. MUNGALA TYPE

a) Geography:

The Mungala is in the region Bandaka, half high-Zaire, May-Dombe Lake, Central Africa, Togo, Chad. The vernacular is Lingala. We then located Mongo, Nkombe, Mbundja, Ekonda, Bansakata, Bakela, Bankutsu, Bayindo the Batetela Topoke of the forest, Lokele, In general: The Mungala is the former citizen of the empire Azade which is why the same traits are in from Buta, Isiro Aketi, Yangambi, Opala, Lomela, Lodja.

The type Mungala consists of a set of actions carried out by trial and error.

The ideal Mungala: Let us first try: Tomeka Naino.

b) In terms of sex:

The Mungala is polygamous, he likes to have many children, causing many partenaitres femmelle; very attached to her partner is a good drageuer; he can marry any woman has, it is more sexual, is the fact of the beverage.

c) In the social point of view:

The Mungala is very social, very open to other foreign groups; phinthrope, masochistic and sadistic at the same time, he drinks a lot, he eats lots of meat, and poison, it is the Zairian more fed, those responsible in nature with the strength blank or there is any.
The Mungala is angry, but not for long, once the conflict evacuated, it is evacuated and ends, but if it has not yet said its last word, there is always a vengeance. The Mungala smokes a little and is orgeuilleux, proud, and bold.

d) In terms of intellectual:

The Mungala was disadvantaged by Nature with its virgin forest implantation, school was late,tha was why, and he is almost fill in. Mais Mungala cultural behavior remains the same to everyone educated or not , they ignore degree; in Mungala there is a kind of like American philosphy , saying that : *Know what you know to do.* Mungala doubt s for everything, especially if he does not know it.

e) In the economic view point:

 Mungala is very materialistic or even megalomaniacal he knows distribute of money ; he loves economic agriculture the commerce, fishing and hunting; he does love to be individualist , does know the cooperatives in business.

f) In political terms:

The Mungala likes the politics, some, disadvantaged by the colonial civilization, he has turned the tide and is capable of political tricks; when Mungala have a conflict between them, if a no Mungala penetrates in, the Bangala unite against the non Mungala, when they finished, they will continue their conflict. They know

dominate their feelings for the group's interest policy, Mungala is very courageous. Mungala in politics, he is often assisted by his wife who drives him still advanced. This is a very important group in Africa or we see the Mungala power in Congo, Central Africa, Togo. In general, the Mungala is a manipulator of other. It has a general less sense of responsibility. Thanks to its ideal; the Mungala has succeeded in many tests; same if he is accused to recognize the method by trial and error ... making wise after.

B. TATU TYPE (KASAIAN)

a.) Geography:

It is located in the Kasai region, north and south of Shaba, we can also find it in South Kivu, Zambia, northern Zimbabwe, some features may be Muluba also in Zulu, and Malawi.

Kasai is the last region created from scratch by the Belgians in 1920. The opinion noted that the entire population is part of Kasai today was part of Shaba, according to the organization of the EIC or ' Independent State of the Kongo (Congo).' This NGO was led by the Germans Otto Von Bismarck of Leopold (Emperor.) We had the region of Shaba, Kivu (Kivu-Kisangani,) Ecuador, and Leopoldville (Banza Kongo.)

We are in the period from 1875 to 1908. Shaba Region stretching from Lake Tanganyika to Ilebo, like in Leopoldville stretched from the Atlantic to Ilebo.

These areas were considered administrative division of the country, as is now the provinces of Kongo churches. These are areas that were part of the Lunda Empire or (FRIENDS' country.) Such that all those traits Bantu, Zambia, Zimbabwe, Malawi, South Africa.

Muluba Type: consists of a set of bold actions, tinted with pride, bravery and exhibition (brave.)

The original Muluba Since Shaba likes hunting, agriculture, and the arts, he was especially motivated by learning, all for self-sufficiency and society.

As he ate his fill, dressed in raffia has his way, he always had a tendency to be proud of what he was and what he did.

The Ideal Muluba: Support with difficulty the foreign domination, but never awarded, it is observation and trying. (Kasai wa belge or Belgium Kasai.) So called because they imitated the Belgium, and got the transfer of technology.

This population is pretending to support the domination of another, but it does not give up, it undertakes the subversive and constructive actions to overthrow his enemy, it often ends up leaving the population to live and do as he wishes , which is the case of the Belgian colonization or those who took power against the Muluba will .

b.) In terms of Intellectual:

The presence of missionaries in Kasai late in the nineteenth century, while Banza Kongo was discovered in the fifteenth century, still has contributed to the training of Luba cadres around Luluabourg (current Kananga,) when starting with Mission Mikalayi , Bunkonde and consort, we saw the Muluba scatter throughout the region and throughout the Kongo, we saw in all regions. The opinion must know that the number of schools in Kasai was far lower than the number of schools in the city of Stanleyville (Kisangani) alone, without counting the Eastern Province where there were many schools. Between 1908 and 1940, Kasai was only plus or minus two primary schools Mikalayi and Bunkonde, which will later emergence of schools and business.

But the population was motivated early for school. We even saw Shabiens brothers, despite numerous schools in the province of Shaba, resistant to go to school, it is that the Muluba at that time believed to have a Culture and Education superior to others, are Belgian them. We saw the same trend in the Luba of Kasai Occidental (The Luluas) resistant to sending their children to school because they thought they were having a superior culture, and thought better educate their children at home instead of school. We see the same trend in the population called native who lived in the villages, not to send children to school, leaving it to the children of the Mission Centres or non-traditional.

The Muluba today is a good school educated in the country, and they know how to use good paper for their life and can even say that after the Bakongo and Bayaka together for the first place in the

Province of Leopoldville, on hesitate for more than Muluba ranks second.

In 1960, members of Leopoldville had already completed six years of secondary education, while members of the Kasai with Wafuana Emery head, had four years averages, and the other for the third and the second side. Muluba among the top graduates of the country, we have technicians of all kinds, even the Belgian were jealous, and they invited Mobutu to prevent Baluba to study at national universities, which try to push for the Moreover adventure school in foreign countries, hence the presence of these frameworks Muluba in foreign countries where their merit is exemplary. Talking about Intelligentsia Kongo in our regions, we must reckon with the presence of one quarter of the intelligentsia Baluba in each region.

c.) In terms of social:

The Muluba is proud of, he is enterprising, resourceful, it follows easily, culture obliges; evil it digests the domination of others, brothers or strangers. He likes emulation, imitation of another to do the same, sometimes exceed, but lets himself go easily to use other means to counter what he calls 'domination.' It is less discreet, it respects the authority when it is strong, considering how the bypass, it is critical, regardless of the authority and is protective from abroad, Luba culture of the family and property. Muluba society is very closed, there is no place for the individual to invent the behavior outside the Custom, which is considered as the law compelling social and sacred, we must do everything according to the custom and tradition, even abroad, the Muluba always refers to the ancestral life. He believes in Witchcraft, the inescapable power of family, the elder law regardless of sex, which he sees as a sacred person, but he knows very little fetishes and magic. The Muluba knows at attained of age what to do from the Birth to Death.

d.) the sexual point of view:

The Muluba can love any woman, of any race or tribe, but its tendency is to love a woman Muluba, which he hopes having already known by his upbringing, all you need to do. The Custom is the author because the parents are doing their work as educators. This education has protected the ancestral Muluba against many bevis disorder and social we saw.

Before 1961, in the city of Luluabourg, a city of seven hundred thousand Inhabitants, only two infirm deaf mutes, no other physical disabilities. In the city of Ngandajika in my youth, I do not known a crippled leg amputated, victim of work railroad BCK

At Mueka, Kakenge, I have had no cripple Physics ... This shows that the laws of the Custom well protected individuals against the evil to come.

The Muluba is able to sacrifice for his wife and family, very jealous of his daughters and his wife, even his mother, as the rival of his father is also hers. It is patrilineal, gives dowry for his marriage before acquiring his wife, the Tradition obliges. This dot is not for sale, but this way to show that we are able to meet the needs to maintain his wife and future family. Once married, the individual must fend husband, although parents are there to help, it still shows how custom through education has enabled him the groom before the wedding, so we ask the husband to show his ability to take care of his wife and his family. Often we think that property or dowry for the marriage must come from the sweat of the brow of her husband's family and husband himself. Never steal money for the dowry, the risk of having children later thieves in the family, where the flight is considered a Crime.

e.) The economic point of view:

The **Muluba** is thrifty, he does not like economic cooperatives as low to cover others, that are likely to live at the expense of others, it is smart, he loves farming, hunting and small businesses, yet he loves small combined with economic foreigners who are not in the village, he likes to work iron, copper and diamonds, he knows these jobs even before the arrival of the Belgian colonialists and Westerners are in, those interests which gives him control attitude of its interests and those of their Western visitors are.
He knows a small artisanal fishing Tushi (eel) and various fish just for family consumption. The dot at the copper Crossett is **(Muluba kanu ya tshombo)** before the currency introduction by the Westerners.

f.) In terms of policy:

The Muluba became as the Roman, weakened by wars of Empire Lunda, Luba, Bayeke, Kasai .. It keeps her pride and arrogance of the achievements of the past, it is easy to use for other services; indiscreet, he can accuse even his own brothers and sisters to win the confidence even pay the other enemies. He knows service to others to show his ability, but think twice to render the same service to his brothers, because he thinks that his brother could exceed. You should know that the Company Luba lives in a competition to do better and earn a lot more than the other, if the Muluba mimics the other is to exceed; not fight against society, but against nature and everyone must work to dominate nature and pure get better, not operating to be exploited by the lazy. When a case arises, the Muluba not hesitate to contribute even to pay more for that evil is dominated, as the Company has no price.

Removed from power by the colonialist, envied by nationals who have yet needs his services, Muluba is not interested in large combined policy. As lack of discretion, today it has a moderate trend. As nationals seem to find the rare bird to get rid of the dictatorship of where it comes from, they tend to push the Muluba to look for what can save the country from its reserves of modern intellectual knowledge.

C. KINOIS TYPE

a) Geography:

Located in Kinshasa, Kinshasa one finds out that this ideal is shared by many people who are outside of Kinshasa. This ideal is shared by all people of all tribes without distinction, but quisont of Kinshasa? This is what NONS will try to explain some types of traits Kinoiserie. We saw Kinshasa, Bukavu, Bandaka, Kisangani, Lubumbashi, Mbuji-Mayi, Kananga, Bandundu and Bas-Zaire kikwite. But these traits are found in lower frequency in some areas than in others; But Kinshasa is the birthplace of Kinoiserie.

KINOISERIE: The set of actions uncertain, impregnated, ignorance, sutureee daring.

The IDEAL Kinshasa: Any attempt to see whether is be done. In the sense that Kinshasa did not need a reason approfondu to cause an action, it does not need to wonder if he knows how or if it does not know, what matters is to ask the act; this to work, so much the better that it fails, too bad. It is actually good or bad consequences past.

Not the Kinshasa Kinshasa Kinshasa Or The exterime of the Left: They are native of Kinshasa, or who have experienced a adolescense kinshasa, but who keeps the moral tribes of origin or the far left Kinshasa . That is to say: Respect for tradition and custom of parents. These are the extremegauche Kinshasa.

b) At intellectually:

The Kinshasa is educated, better informed because he even has a degree in Kinshasa says nothing, it can be a good technician, but he will love easily acts bold, unscrupulous. The Kinshasa ignores the serious, the course, the social. Kinshasa contains all the best schools in the country, the school have safe form of intellectual values, but of conscience on the cheap. Those who have studied in these schools, without sharing the ideal of Kinshasa are reliable values .. We shall see out of St. Raphael, St. George ... who diregent healthy countries. The ones that do that Kinshasa's wife extremegauche not the ideal common, and were regarded by all as shy.

c) In terms of office:

The Kinshasa does not longremps angry, he does not racune, he fights rarely there is much talk, even cry, he knows the other out of Petrin, he smokes a lot, including hemp, he drinks a lot and it's fun and funny and he loves music and dance, recreation, entertainment, sleeping anywhere, Kinshasa is the simple, individualistic, malicious, grimacing, dishonest sometimes clever, cheater; it is by trial and error; Kinshasa is pedant and rash, he loves corruption.

d) In terms of Sex:

The Kinshasa is a great sex; this is sexual relations at all, but not a true love in these reports because the Kinshasa is not often the good fortune to partner; The sexuality is for an act of snobbery Kinshasa; adolescents imitate adults because they have seen the last act, they do not know the reason for marriage; many conjugal unions are not official divorce as it wants and renconcilie is in delay etc. Many miners are already fathers unofficial. Is accentuated by the sexuelite: various leisure that has lacated kinshasa.

D. MUKONGO TYPE

a) Geography:

The type is in the Mukongo regnen Lower Zaire, in the primitive areas of Kinshasa, Masina. Ndjili, Kingasani, Kimbaseke, Makala Mbumbu, Selembao. Type Mukongo: Consists character has a fuzzy, contradictory, and apparently segregationist shy.

Ideal Mukongo: Mikammia Mbwa: The weight of the dog: The dog's weight will a single score. That is to say: for all of the Bakongo. The fact of not being of the ancient kingdom of Congo, one can not enter into the intimate sphere of Bakongo, even if we approach a non Mukongo, that's all dimplement to use as a means and not as an element constitif group.

b) In terms of Intellectual:

The Mukongo type is the most learned of the Republic since the 15th century, but the Belgian colonization slows Mukongo had to wait that other not yet learned they were inflicting mental retardation four century (see 15eS. If leaves on the intellectual Mukongo, who until the other has been the first bishop besides that of the S 15E, the first professor of the University, the First President of the republic, the medium had favors This rise also, we had even during the colonial era, the best schools of the Republic, the University had Commenee home, the colony school Boma Kinsantu, Banana, Matadi ... are major centers that provide training to many Cade today. Statistically schools of Lower Zaire exceed in numbers cele> other areas.

c) In terms of sex:

The Mukongo knows an intra-clan marriage; crossbred cousins can marry. True love is in the Mukongo-Mukongo in a woman who is highly regarded and appreciated. The rest Mukongo stays long time unmarried, it is often to wait for the cousin or the niece who is still young, Mukongo is less authoritarian on children who are not afraid of the maternal uncle, and he can marry to everyone, but marriage will not be easily accepted by the family, even if it tolerates. The Mukongo is very authentic in sex, but on him, he does not lose his head in love, he is timid, because it is not these, he often left to see another really not the case, and it often leaves the other to see how this really he wantes.

d) In the social point of view:

 The Mukongo still doubts its relations with other non-Bakongo, the east trusting himself, he hesitated a lot before relying on someone where the alleged timidity, this attitude is simply a method of approach, he studied, reasons, examines how and why ... before enter in contact with each other; the Mukongo is, apparently calm, but on a fighter and he knows how to choose the means and the subjects are in reports. Even with other Mukongo, it yank not directly, he hesitates ... and acts. The Mukongo opponent is a very strong and very cunning he is enterprising, introverted and a heavy smoker; much Pendent smoking through the nose, he likes corruption.

e) In the economic point of view:

the Mukongo is the only zairian which has exploited its rich first of all the only regions to have great centers region having bank branches Dan, centre touts many banks are at the bottom represented in Bas-Zaire in their discretion. Bakongo love agriculture and trade, possess better Farms of all species of grand store, wholesale and retail down as Kinshasa Bas-Zaire has the best facilities than in Shaba to view plants that better number or quality.
 Mukongo the carrier, he is the best transporter, mostly routed path connecting and so the great petit villages. Mukongo nests of the best to have the road infrastructures, the best of the Republic. Seeing the economic development of the region of Low Zaire. All Republic had worked for her since then, but until colonization, Mukongo has a great initiative and aimed worker.

E. MUYAKA TYPE

a) Geography

Muyaka type is in the Bandundu region, we can find the same traits of appearance at Tshikapa, Mueka, Dekese. They are the same residents at Kwilu, Idiofa, Dekese, Tshikapa of Mueka and around Kinshasa.

Muyaka Type: Consists of a series of bold and firm actions. These are people who do not let themselves be, they are ready to intervene and decide the course of history. One should know that Muyaka is a strain of the 'old youth soldier' of EMPIRE LUNDA. Parents continued military education to their children. The Bayaka are in Bandundu as a result of war against the Portuguese soldiers and their allieds from Boma, and consort Kinsantu, which were in the Province of Banza Kongo.

b.) In terms of Intellectual:

Muyaka type is highly educated by the action of Catholic missionaries, especially the Jesuits in Bandundu. These missionaries have made Bandundu a nursery intellectuals as Mukongo his cousin, who took advantage of the presence of

Catholic missionaries in the province of Leopoldville and Lower River for training. Muyaka uses the well educated graduate in life. It is well known, see the difference between the educated and uneducated. The intellectual Muyaka do not let it go, he likes the discussion, he is skeptical, he defends his rights against wind and marshes.

c.) In terms of social

The Muyaka is secured, he likes to act as a group, very skeptical, he drinks enough, quiet and talkative without saying openly secrets; he is lucid, he is angry and ready to act, very open, it comes into contact with anyone and even defeated, he does not let his principles he holds much; he likes the war, likes agriculture and commerce, he smokes enough, he believes in witchcraft and magic or fetishes.

d.) In sexual terms:

It was matrilineal, children followed the mother line, represented by the maternal uncle, he can marry any individual from any tribe, provided that the Maternal Uncle accepts the union, if contrary, very disciplined Muyaka abandons the Contract. He is unstable in each union in love, even in marriage, because it can give more children with a woman, provided it is not responsibility for children. The only stable marriage that is contracted with the paternal aunt's daughter will give children to her brother, who is considered "Maternal uncle" entitled children, biological father of her nephew, husband of her daughter, mother of children. If he marries another woman of any tribe, he abandons the children went to benefit the family of his wife, and the marriage did not last.

Today, Thanks to Abolish Matriacat by President Mobutu, the Muyaka people marry, the children follow the paternal line, and weddings are starting to become stable and parents responsible of their children. Previously it was the maternal uncle who had the responsibility for all the children of his sisters, on behalf of the family.

e.) the economic point of view:

The Muyaka is a good trader, he knows saving a lot like his cousin Mukongo; economic scams he knows, he likes trading cooperatives, and he is capable of economic cooperation.

f.) In terms of political

The Muyaka as Muluba, Mukongo and other tribes from Empire Lunda have some squeals policies from Lunda Empire.He was the basis for the creation of the militant youth of the Lunda Empire in Banza Kongo (United Kingdom's). Based on these effects, he is capable of many political tricks. He knows how to defend the public cause, whatever the price. He has always the political principles, he knows how to keep the political discretion if necessary, he is a formidable opponent, he loves political discretion, he knows conduct a political debate to the end, he TREND Revolutionary.

F. Swahili TYPE

a. Geography:

Swahili type is found in the region of Kivu, the WEST of Rwanda, Burundi and Northern. The same features are found in Shaba, Zaire and Upper.
As these features are in Tanzania, Kenya and Somalia, but all Swahili both of these countries are present as Zaire, in the sense that they are much more marked by their original features, while the Zairian possess a quarter. This is due to purely Zaire character brand dominates in Zaire in general. While other foreign, of having penetrated the Kongo, influenced some of the Zairian their character brought to Zaire, where they had immigrated during the raid Arabized of Zanzibaris.
Type the Swahili is a set of concrete actions based on personal effort sharing with others. This ideal is often: "work for the welfare of the Community. "

b) In terms of Intellectual:

The Swahili is much educated, that the presence of the Marist missionaries who had taken education Upper Zaire and Kivu. It has all the frames needed and are at ease with views of other regions. The Muswahili used both graduated in everyday life to its penetration into the society and even influences society. Graduating to a certain social value, it is used well in society. The instruction is well suited to local life, educated and uneducated coexist in perfect harmony, the last benefit advice early to properly conduct their business.

c) From the social point of view:

Swahili is quiet, we often prefer to call 'Swahili' instead of any short Swahili, because the majority of the population not only speaks Swahili is a Arabized language, led by the Zanzibaris, rather they speak the local languages and in a variety of tribal populations, Swahili is a common trait caused by Arabized foreigns.

He is disciplined in the sense that when it is necessary, and not when it is not, he takes out his reactions to the circumstances, it is reserved and moderate. Indeed, he still loves his Mwamis village and tribes, he loves the community and able to sacrifice for others. He drinks a lot, believe in fetishes, and Witchcraft, it is a great worker.

d) the sexual point of view:

It is capable of true love, like polygamy, often like Swahili woman, he rarely believes in marriage with women from other parts of the Kongo (Zaire ;) he is able to sacrifice for his wife and children, it is fun in love, laugh, he laughs and wowed her with talk that panicked many women.

e) From the economic point of view:

Swahili phone is shopper, he loves farming, he knows how economic cooperatives, made combined business, he likes to win a lot and spend moderately, it obeys the laws of economics easily as it sees its interests at stake otherwise reject it all, and ready to revolt, often it protects and abuse at the same time corruption by the local and national economy. The presence of foreign Rwandans in their region (Kivu) was much disturbed the stability of their economy.

f) The political point of view:

The Muswahili likes politics, from the Lunda Empire, it is set between palaver regions Borders, it is seasoned, progressive and has a revolutionary trend, and indeed there has been a lot since Soumialot and Kabila and Mayi Mayi , Mulele until today, it looks like it is marked by incessant political wars. The Muswahili has played many roles in the Country politics, it is feudalized and Federalist.

G. SHABIAN TYPE

a) Geography.:

The type Shabian is in Shaba Region, in southern Zambia, northern Zimbabwe,
East Grand Kasai to Mwena Ditu,Tshimbulu, Mweka Kakenge,
due to the influence of the Society of Railway BCK, and One can find its points of
resemblance in South Africa, Malawi and Mozambique. This is due to the fact that
most of the current immigration Kongolese went South to North Africans.
The type Shabian is brutal and stubborn actions, often little thought.
The ideal Shabian is ' Ni bure, fwanya yako!' 'Is nothing, go ahead' can be
translated into Swahili As the Americans would say: 'Just do it!'

b) In terms of Intellectual.:

The Shabian loves very little education, and work, those who work and honor of
Shaba came from other provinces, especially the Kasai, which one is jealous
today. Also noteworthy is the influence of Zanzibaris Mwami Muenda Munongo
said Katanga of Bungeya for the job half done. Life was also facilitated by the
presence of many Western societies in the province, in search of the hands of
cheaper works.
The Shabian is taught today by the political influence which prompted the young
Shabians for studies, once formed by any professional school, he keeps his
service, even up to his death, he easily called 'Mutoto ya BCK is, there Mining
Union etc.. 'i.e. the child or BCK, Meaning Union, 'to say that he lives, works and
dies for the BCK or The Union Meaning.' The Opinion emphasized that, all who
swear in the name of co Shaba companies, are still not originate in Shaba, but
they came from everywhere, and they will be called 'BA MUANA SHABA,' and all
consider themselves as brothers and sisters, all black and white speak Swahili.
The Shabian knows to use his degree for life and it is rare that Shabian easily

exchange business, he still prefers to keep the same job, the companies have contributed to the education of children of workers before going to engage others to Moreover, in many societies, their staff Frames (direction) is composed of the children of workers, Umba Kya Mitala who studied with the Gécamines scholarship, became Minister of Mines and CEO. It was the policy of the settlers in Kongo, as we have seen Tambwe Mwamba Kivu, Pay Pay (Quincaina) and consort, sons of workers whose education was paid by the companies, became managers of these companies. Tambwe Muamba further claimed that *'Zaire Tin' Kindu was the company of his father. Sic!*

c) the sexual point of view:

The Shabian is given enough love, but it separates the work and love, he never confuses the two, he does not like polygamy, the job requires, because workers know a lot of frequent job transfers; That is why monogamy saves him a lot of hassle of several households. The Shabians always loves in the same camps with the youth of the same company, there was even a great rivalry between the companies, this resulted in the same loves and marriages, children BCK did want to marry with the BCK girls, it was the same for other companies or companies, they laughed a lot of spouses brought from villages who married in camps or cities of Shaba. The Muana Shaba from Kasai, preferred marriage the Muana Shaba girl, whatever their provincial origin to marry another spouse that came freshly to Shaba province; companies encouraged the movement, in some companies, managers ME *(hands of indigenous works)* recorded marriages between young husband on behalf of the Civil State. The conflict Kasai-Shaba was born there. While the Kasai was part of Shaba stretching from Lake Tanganyika to ILEBO, the confluence of the Kasai River and the Lulua River until 1920 when it retired to the Shaba Lubilash, next to City Luputa.

d) From the social point of view:

The Shabian commonly called 'MUANA SHABA' like camaraderie, sport and play, we will see later that the best players come from Zairian Shaba, among the children of workers, again companies were based, as they maintained much sport in society. Luluabourg won the provincial capital through sport (football) winning against Lusambo, former Capital of Kasai, by 3 goals to 1 in 1949, on that date, the provincial Capital will be transferred to Luluabourg until nowK; the players made the victory came from Shaba, where they worked in the BCK transferred to Luluabourg, they were lined up to play against Lusambo, and they signed the final victory.

The Shabian loves and still loves in Shaba, although unemployed, it was difficult to convince the player-TP Mazembe and Lupopo (BCK) to keep playing Kinshasa. Shaba players sold their houses given to Leopards for victory by President Mobutu to go buying other houses in Shaba.

The Shabian is stubborn and obstinate, he is right or he is wrong, he defended his actions vehemently. It is focused on the Shaba, he does not see in other regions, nor their importance, it is always Shaba that matters is also an area that has gained much industrial development, the number of established plants in the province, but be aware that the indigenous population has not won anything in all this, because even the sport was an interest in the Belgian who ran everything, When intellectuals Shabians wanted to say a word, they were reduced to silence, s If they insist they are put in prison. Like most intellectuals were Shabians Kasaians, Belgian began to preach anti Kasai tribalism they left a Munongo Tchombe consort and, later, they will transmit the tribal doctrine practiced in Shaba President Mobutu who will its workhorse with MPR.

The Shabian is helpful, easily won the esteem of others, brutal, it is less evil in his actions than other non Shabians, he loves the white man, he sings well, he even suggests that "Muzungu or mungu, "which says:" White is god. "What disturbed the other tribes of the Kongo was nicknamed Manzikala Governor, who had Upper Zaire as a liberator of Shaba, forcing White to let blacks into public facilities reserved for whites only. The price was heavy by the Governor, for the power of Kinshasa (Mobutu) was pro-Belgian. Despite the death of a Belgian, much was done, all facilities were open to all the world including black.

This aspect of 'Muzungu' was mostly seen by the natives in the industrial aspect of the Shaba colonialists realized 'Shaba' who could not envy the West in this aspect.

e) From the economic point of view:

The Shabian likes the manual work than office work (maybe, due to its insufficient studies.) He loves agriculture, very little trade, it is not capable of the combined economic work, he likes to be ordered order, corruption is not shabian there cannot by the work he has everything, he does not like taking advantage of others. He considers himself rich forever, for the Shaba is rich, they said: "Katanga wa madi," which says: "Shaba rich."If Kongo loses Industry Shabian so modern, we must conclude that the USA has lost California. Some scholars think.

f) The political point of view.:

Muana Shaba is adamant in its actions and policy decisions. It is and will always act in the same way, even without success, he has a peerless political courage, but courage is due to lack of sufficient thought before acting and is very bold opponent, he has to anyone except the Muzungu, it does not change, it takes in the political discussion the expertise of youth shabian, considered Shabian, for youth was educated in the spirit of Shaba rich and strong, what is lacking in that other Kongolese do not see the ground, but foreign policy doctrines. He does everything for the group by the group and in the group. It is because of this idea that the Belgian did not tolerate Tchombe changing the Basic Law, the Constitution of Luluabourg and later Ngunza speaking group (Kongo,) when they were in business in Kinshasa, they will conveyed the idea of Muana Shaba (Spirit Group or Company) other Kongolese. The Belgian wanted to exploit the people with the notion of group-company, but never help the people use to enjoy his wealth. Hence the preference of Mobutu (selfish false Mungala) has Tchombe by the Belgian.

The Shabian is not tribalist, the Muana Shaba means that any child or adult who has experienced companies Shabian Education at school, at work, in youth groups, camps for workers in the vocational training centers ... All who reacts violently without thinking too much and think "Muzungu or mungu. "Often lives in Shaba yetu that says (. Our Shaba)

Despite the political will of some leaders Shabians the Muana Shaba is and remains Shabian because it embodies morality, Labor and expertise Shabian that non Shabians did not. Moral of this group and its interests was brought by the elders of the Lunda Empire, reinforced by the Belgian military, Charter Colonial Caroline, the French Girl-Friend of King Leopold II and Belgian companies Metropolis selfish; envied by the Portuguese (Gyungu wa ku Mwanza, false famous leader Katanga,) as if we were on the road to the oracle Brazilian. This morality is the set of legacy and lived by the old black holders of these brutal highways, companies have taught the children, the youth has internalized the population has lived and integrated, hence the Muana Shaba or Spirit Shabian Group.

CHAPTER TWO: DO YOU KNOW ZAIRIAN WOMEN?

For this study, we classify women according to their comportments difference: the ideals from these women feel situated in interregional aries, and find the women with a different aspects; different woman had other combinations of features with other ... this is the case of the Baluba from Kinshasa, Bangala in Kasai, the Bakongo in Shaba. Thus, therefore, these types regroup women in Mungala, kisangani woman, Mukongo woman, kinshasa woman, Muluba woman, shaba woman, Kwilu and Swahili woman, without taking care of their original tribes.

1. Kasai Woman or Mamu

a) Geography:

She lives in the region of the Kasai, they are Lulua, the Baluba of Kasai, Bakete, balualua, babindi, basonge; all regions of Kabinda, Lubao, muena-Ditu, kanintshina, Luiza, Tshikapa Luebo demba, Dibaya, kazumba, Tshikapa Kakenge, Tshilenge, Miabi, Dimbelenge, Mashala, bena-dibela, Lusambo mpania Mutombo, Bakua Mputu Ngandajika, part of muena-Ditu.

b) In terms of sex:

The Muluba is in love, submissive, grimacing, apparently faithful, can marry anyone, quite feminine and female. Able sacrifice of love for their spouse or children, and allene all for the love and the one she loves.

c) In the social perspective:

Women Muluba is cooperating, less malignant, obedient, quiet, low cunning, feminine enough, fearful, often hypocritical, she does not drink much, drunkenness is rare for her. Maternal and reproductive health and founder of the New Family, his family.

d) In the economic point of view:

It is almost non-materialistic and it does not bind the material social life, she can live with everyone and is quite resourceful; the economy belongs to her husband and his family; incapable of hard work.

e) In political terms:

The woman Muluba ignores politics, she does not want political tricks; she loves love above all else and is often the victim of polique, that is to say, that it can be politically without exploition namely, it no ambition pouvoirmuluba not, the woman participates in power, but does not exercise it; c is what created this almost caracttere of disinterestedness in modern politics.

f) In terms of intellectual:

The Muluba is intellectual. It uses well his degree in social life, but sometimes husbands prevent their wives to work; Baluba women who work are often single. But the situation is changing more and more because of the modern societies.

2. Mungala Woman or Muan'a Mayi.

a) Geography:

It is often found in the Region of the Equator, Mayi-Dombe, Bandundu city, Opala, Sankuru, Isiro, Kole, Lomela, Dekese, we can say that most feel the Mongo, Gombe, Bunja, Ggwandi, Gbuaka, Konda, Bansakata, Tetela, Bambele, and many other ethnic groups, who are in the region of Equator.....

b) In terms of studies:

The Mungala does very few studies; sometimes not, even some give more; we find popular and indigenous Alerts between many scholarized population than elsewhere.

C) The sexual point of view:

She has great pity for men, she offers herself easily to men; it is in the first raw for exciting and can marry elesewhere. No imperturbable race, not tribes with interference for loving; she ignores fidelity and is pleasant and not lovely, even she likes sex taking; often she has some social and public mannerism.

d) In the social perspective:

She is very philanthropic, lucid and outgoing and is open to others regardless of race or tribe and is impesante, gossip and cunning, she drinks a lot.

e) In the economic point of view:

The Muana-a-Mayi is very materialistic,   debrouillard and commercantelle, can enrich his husband back without thoughts, its materiality does not condition his sexuality, who feels separated and whose common point is rare.

f) In terms of policy:

Muana-a-Mayi is very sensitive to the political, does not like to do it herself, she handles the husband, the Compains, friends, ... camarades for lancher in politics and realize their dreams; this has repoud his extroverted character; Sybian her when she drives men to implement their agenda policies. Mungala wily woman, is a good political inspiration. At this point of view, can be said that the success of many Bangala is due to the courage of their women politically. This political servitude may be given to Mungala as tribut. But her political inspiration is not for Organization, it is just to maintain a social climate round her and for her.

3. Kisangani woman or Semeki

a) Geography:

It is in the center of high zaire, in the sub-regions of tchiope, Isangi, Yangambi yatelema, yangambi and other regions round the capital of Haut- Zaire. This often feels Lokele, babuwa , topoke, Bamanga ... and all small gastritis surrounding these major tribes sometimes Bambole forming a different type of kisangani, because Opala is near the Bangala People that are their origin tribe, but When their stay in Kisangani, they become the best of Semeki Women .

b) The intellectual point of view:

 Kisangani woman is cultivated; the many semeki have a degree, but they are attached to life and its vicissitudes. Thus does not have a value whit her degree in social disploma that has only a honnorific value.

c) In sexual point of view:

The semeki is flattering, cheater sollicitous, and suddenly loaded by any partner for mood and is just lovely for marriage, that has no import that to her, can import of any tribe or race, but has condion to stay in Kisangani or environmt (top zamre); she toleres with difficulties the Village of her husband who is not from Boyoma; even married, the semeki ignores the reliabilities.

Semeki (continued)

d) For the social point of view:

Semeki is the cunning, introvert and extrovert at the same time that is to say: she looked outside to meet its own needs; egeistement helpful and is very intuitive, can penetrate and reach the intentions of sen interlecuteur easily; she drinks a lot.

e) In the economic point of view:

The semeki is materialist, she confuses the materiality and love; it is the same condition for an old sexual love, or that begins, or is in its infancy. She likes   trading, and agriculture.

f) In political terms:

The semeki is very sensitive to politics and is a Nationalist woman in politics, she likes to play herself within the political power, she is ambitious, may oppose even her own husband or her brother in politics.

4. Mukongo woman or Maman Fioti

a) Geography:

It is in all of Lower Kongo (Zaire) region and primitive areas of Kinshasa. It is women who are found along railway Kinshasa-Matadi, Boma, Tshiela, Banana, Selembao, binza, makala, masina, Kingasani, bumbu, njili, Maluku, the nord of Angola and sud of the Congo . Not to be confused with the woman's other tribes who live in these urban areas, but who do not share the same ideal. In general the Mukenge woman comes from the ancient kingdom of Congo.

b) In terms of sex:

Maman fioti does like the Mukongo in general, and his cousin by excellence and can marry a no Mukongo with difficulty, it is a problem of marriage; she falls rarely in love with other tribes; their marriage is often within the clan, and between cousins and nephews, in the name of mama fioti marriage is to get back the parental blood. Even President Mobutu abolished the Matriarchy, Maman Fioti thinks, she is still in.

c) In the social perspective:

The Mukongo woman is hypocrite, apparently fresh and feminine too, authoritarian and cunning and is taditionalist and conservative, sighted and mischievous. The mama fioti sees only the interest of his own family, which is why a no Mukongo husband who is not cousin or nephew, always has problems with her flair, she does apprehend the feelings of others by flattery; she smokes a lot .

d) Intellectual stand point:

The maman fioti is very educated, she uses her degree as a valid name; able to defend herself intellectually as we ought to put in front of the man without complexes.

f) In the economic point of view:

The maman is very materialistic; it does not confus the heritage with that of being wife and resourceful worker; she also prefers the agricultural trade.

e) In political terms:

Maman fioti ambitions power, she loves the exercise for herself, she may take sides against her husband or any relative; she knows how to make calculations succeed; surpring, she knows the others; also uses some means to succeed and she is rarely look at her husband or partner that they love to be able to support herself, if she is less educated, she does not venture so much. But she knows to speculate for her succees.

5. Kinshasa Woman or la Kinoise

A) Geography:

The woman lives in the city of Kinshasa, but there are some who live in the city without Sharing the Kinshasa ideal.

b) Intellectually:

Apparently Kinoise woman is intellectual for her, it is her business; the studies are tricks to penetrate into society, but not a cultural value; and can complete the studies with many dishonest means, but deep down she does not know anything, there are about 48 percent of illiterate in Kinshasa, Alert, the middle where they live is not conduciving to analphebetism.

c)The sexual point of view:

The Kinshasa knows no love and is key to everything, or incapable of true love, it's fun, grimacing, little obaissante, unfaithful, she can marry anyone, the service at her wedding is only adventure ; when she had some relations with a boyfriend, he became by the very fact her husband, she "multiple husbands of the same kind, and is often unstable marriage less feminine and lack of charm, she does not know the difference between the husband and kind 'amant na ngai;' the bizareries of Kinshasa make her a woman who excites least, that's why many men come running behind the under age girls who are not much older contaminers by, for once with of kinoiseries, we abandon them for other underage girls, say some men.

d) In the social perspective:

The Kinoise is misleading, malicious, trucheuse, pedantic, capricious, ambitious and capable of betrayal, daring, fun, gossip and dishonest. When she entered into relations w ith someone is to hurt tomorrow, so she is very skeptical about nothing, she does not know anything Alers, and seek to know nothing. She has no pity, it does not inspire either pity, she can drink it right.

e) In the economic point of view:

She is resourceful enough, megalomaniac, she wants to be a lot of assets that may not necessary; thrifty months, she lives from day to day; recently became the Kinshasa shopping, but his character has any key, lets see it is a businesswoman, while this is not, in reality it is a false air as it gives it a good grimacing. Desire to have soneconomie next to that of her boyfriend or husband.

f) In political terms:

She aspires to power, it can combine for power, often it makes for the power and can take a stand against such na ye, her husband, her brother ... it can take power and can take power, but as luis seems and can take any party, not because it's good, but because he likes; it takes to satisfy her feelings and not the interests of any kind, she has no sense of responsibilites.

6. Women Shaba Woman or la Shabienne.

a) Geography:

it is in the Shaba region, South Kivu, Zambia and South, the Ngandajike.Luiza ... they are Balubakat, Bemba, Lunda Kanyoka, some groups in Kasai Oriental bene Mukuna (bena tshitolo, kalonji katshibanda) and some groups Lulua Kaai at Western (bene tshitol, kalonji Tshibanda ka) and some groups in luluba kasi occidentel (ben Tshibanda ka); ill should be noted that in both this type of woman kasia shabienne dimune gradually, and some features noted in some individuals sefont .

b) the sexual point of view:

she is in love can Sacrafice female spouse, she can marry anyone has apparammenrt faithful concervatrice gentle and calm. And traditional.

c) The social point of view:

The timorous shabian is apparently calm, respectful, respective, less malignant obedient, little more Cooperating she drinks enough.

Not sensitive to it considering all the materialism economy belongs to her husband she loves agriculture.

e) The political point of view:

senseble policy has not, she prefers to let the men do the politque politque is the affair of the men tradialnolmellement shabianne participart to power but does not expercait or abndon today.

f) The intellectual point of view:

She loves enough intellectual etubes worth to be noted that the shabienne was disadvantaged by the middle for his first INSRUCTION of schools for girls were rare entait it the same for the Muluba who had the advantage of aviore abandons its middle traditional.

7. Kongolese Eastern Woman or Bibi

a) Geography:

The region of Kivu, eastern Zaire high, Kindu, Wagenia Ubundu Kasongo, some tribes of North shaba.cesont for most of the Bakusu, bashi Barega, Bamanga, Kasongo and some border tribes deRuandaetBurundi, Tazanie, Kenya, Unganda

b) In terms of sex:

The bug is in love substantially, too feminine and charming, she ignores the fidelity can marry anyone who has, in addition to her husband, she has a series of lovers she does not tend to hide; but it still retains the love of her husband, she is able to sacrifice her children for her husband. With his natural charm that seems, the bug is able to excite any man Manly.

c) In social terms:

She shy, resourceful, grimacing, Cooperating very capable of sacrifice for others than she drinks a lot, quiet and gentle.

d) In terms of intellectual:

Swahili woman is highly educated, she knows to use his knowledge in social life, studies have valued the cultural certainty.

e) In terms of Economic:

She knows materialism based goods for society and not to impose; The economy is guaranteed by the man who apparently owns, she loves agriculture.

f) In political terms:

It is sensitive to politics, but it does not aim the power, rather it leaves men exercise power although she participated in political life.

<h1 style="text-align:center">8. Kwilu Woman or Maman leki</h1>

a) Geography:

The leki mom is in the Bandundu region, especially along the river Kwilu, Idiofa, part of Tshikapa, Dibaya-Lubo, Ilebo Mueka, northern Lower Zaire. They are right on Bayanji, Bapende, Bakuba, Bashilele, Bayaka, Batandu, and most of the tribes that are located along the river Kwilu.

b) Intellectually:

The Kwiloise woman is very intellectual, it even beats the record in Zaire, it is not the cultural value of his degree, in many cases, it competes with men she likes to use his degree in everyday life.

c) In terms of sex:

She's in love, marry anyone can easily, do not alliene interts has his love, love is more intellectualized than sentimental, she shares the love and material interests; incapable of sacrifices for her husband or her children.

d) In terms of office:

THE Kwiloise is cunning, reserved, gossip, and some Cooperating absolutist secrecy she knows, like her sister Mukongo; when she enters a society is to play a role, not to assist others. It can cooperate to realize the common interests and is also authoritarian she drinks enough.

e) In the economic point of view:

Resourceful, materialistic, she likes to work alone or in groups for certain interests realize. The economy is for her or her children, she often combines its economy to that of man.

f) In political terms:

She likes politics, her ambition is power, but the company is kwiloise hard it can break easily, we will see it play important roles in the mass political meetings she loves, and she is free of the responsibility.

MVIDIE MUKULU OU KOLE MUKOLE

BENDE (ADAM)

MBUYI TSHIAME (EVE)

KOLE –A-BAYEMBI

KOLE-A-TSHILONDA

KOLE MUANA

KOLE TSHIFUKILE   ....   **KOLE W0T0**

SHABA	**EQUATEUR**
KASAI	**BANDUNDU**
BANDUNDU	**KASAI**
	HAUTKONGO
BANZAKONGO	**BANZAKONGO**
BATEKE	**BOLOBO**
KIVU	
HAUTKONGO	

BENA KOLE

BIBLIOGRAPHIE

Psychopolitique: Mbangu Mangala 1972-2012

Psychosociale: Mbangu Mangala wa Mangala, 1980-2013

Psychologie Générale: Cours de professeur Vanove, Lovanium 1965

Psychologie sociale: Professeur Kanga Kalemba Vita, ULC 1972.

Dynamique pédagogique: Professeur Bikayi Obel, ULC 1972.

Histoire du Kongo Corrigée: Mbangu Mangala, 2014.

Auteur Mbangu Mangala,

Il naquit au Kasaï, le 20 Décembre, l'an 1945.

Des parents modestes, il débutera ses études primaires à la mission catholique Tshikula, et au centre scolaire rural de Kamuandu; il finira sa formation scolaire primaire à Kanyama, province du Shaba,

Il termina les secondaires à Luluabourg, Kasaï Occidental. Il est ancien des Collèges St Georges à (Ngandajika), Pie X (Kananga), et de l'Athénée de Luluabourg (Section Normale). Il fera des universités à Lovanium, à l'UOC (Shaba), et à ULC (Kisangani).

Il décrocha un titre en Psychologie et en Education, comme licencié.

Il travaillera au Ministère de l'Education nationale pour une période de trente ans, il occupera tous les échelons de ce Département : Enseignant au Secondaire, de l'attaché de bureau au Directeur du Département pendant plus de quinze ans. On l'appellera souvent Conseiller.

Il participera à beaucoup de conférences internationales et missions officielles dans le Monde, il animera la Radio scolaire et plusieurs directions du Département de l'Education Nationale.

Depuis 1995, il vit aux USA, où il a été Visiting Scholar à Harvard University pour deux ans ; il parachèvera ses études en accrochant le titre américain de Master in Education. Il s'occupe maintenant des recherches dans beaucoup d'Universités américaines dans le cadre de Doctorant en Management.

Il est marié à Tshituka Angel Mbangu, et il est père de plus de dix enfants.